Welsh Speed Kings

Robin and Chris Lawrie
Illustrated by Robin Lawrie

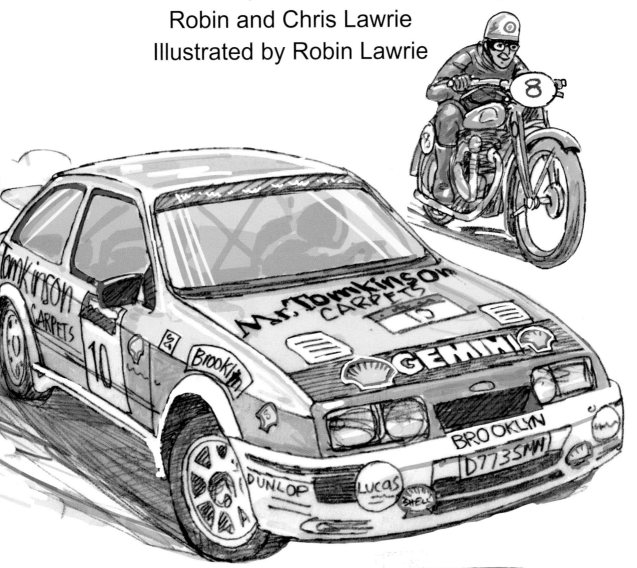

Carreg Gwalch

First published in 2011

Published with the financial support
of the Welsh Books Council

ISBN: 978-1-84527-353-8

Cover design: Sion Ilar/Welsh Books Council
Cover illustration: Robin Lawrie

Design: Chris Lawrie

Published by Gwasg Carreg Gwalch,
12 Iard yr Orsaf, Llanrwst, Wales LL26 0EH
tel: 01492 624031
fax: 01492 641502
email: books@carreg-gwalch.com
internet: www.carreg-gwalch.com

Printed and published in Wales

Contents

JOHN PARRY THOMAS

Carstruck!

It was a warm spring day in Oswestry, in 1899, and John Parry Thomas, known as Parry, was walking from his boarding school to the sweet shop. He was in a bad mood and needed cheering up. His exam results had been bad and the English lads at school had been teasing him again, calling him 'Bullocks One' because he was Welsh and comes from Bwlchycibau – a name they couldn't pronounce.

Suddenly, he heard a big commotion, the clattering hooves of startled horses, dogs barking. A red shape appeared at the end of the high street, coming towards him, fast. It's a car! Young Parry Thomas thought it must be doing at least 20 miles per hour! A Benz Velo, great-great-grandfather of today's Mercedes-Benz, the first one he'd ever seen. The driver stopped right in front of him, pulled off goggles and gloves and walked into the chemist's shop behind him. Parry stared at the beautiful machine.

A few minutes later the driver came out carrying a large bottle of petrol, which you could only buy at a chemist's shop in those days. He poured it into the car's fuel tank. The aroma of hot engine oil and petrol hit Parry Thomas's nose and he was hooked. Forever.

He knew in a second that this was his future and the future of the new century that was about to begin. Instead of buying sweets, Parry went into the newsagent and bought a copy of *The Autocar*. It would be his favourite magazine for the rest of his life.

By the time 'lights out' was called in the school dormitory that night he had read it from cover to cover. Parry Thomas's passion for cars was to last all his life.

London

Parry Thomas studied hard at school from then on. He knew he had to if he was going to make his dream of working with cars come true. In 1902, he was accepted to study at the City and Guilds College in London.

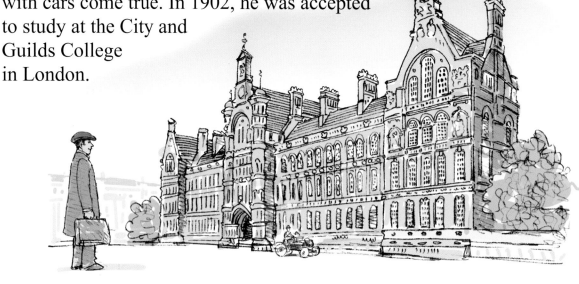

Everywhere he looked on the capital's busy streets there were cars of all shapes and sizes, but they were all noisy, smelly and slow. Parry's head buzzed with ideas of how he could improve them, but first he would need a workshop.

He decided to pay a visit to his mother to ask for her help.

Parry had to wait until after he had graduated before his mother gave him enough money to set up a workshop full of everything he needed for his research. He'd noticed the terrible crunching noises that cars made when their drivers changed gears. He knew gear-changing could be improved so he set about inventing an automatic transmission.

It worked but, sadly, it was too heavy to be used in cars.

However, it worked well in lorries, trains and buses.

Over the next few years, the ideas kept coming – air brakes (the hissing noise you hear from big lorries when they stop), torsion bars and anti-sway bars, which are all still used on modern cars. Every time one of these inventions was used on a vehicle, a little money – a royalty – was paid to Parry Thomas.

Brooklands

Then came his biggest challenge. Leyland wanted him to build 'the world's best car' as a rival to the Rolls Royce. It was to be the world's first supercar. Parry Thomas knew he could do it. The result was the

Leyland 8. It was fast and beautiful but was very, very expensive, and only fourteen were ever built. Two were bought by an Indian Maharaja, and a factory mechanic had to go out to India to teach the Maharaja's mechanics how to service them because they were

so complicated. Another was bought by Irishman Michael Collins, then Commander in Chief of the Irish Army, who was ambushed while on the way to a meeting during the Civil War and was shot dead in it in August 1922.

The lack of sales disappointed Leyland and Parry Thomas resigned from the company. But he must have left on good terms because they let him keep one of the cars, as well as lots of spare parts.

Soon afterwards, he bought a house with a new workshop at the Brooklands racing circuit near London. This was where all the car racing action was in the first part of the twentieth century. Built in 1907, the steeply-banked track was the world's first car racing circuit, and one of the first airports.

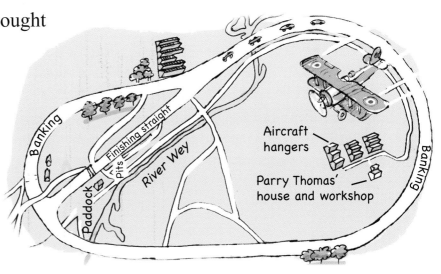

The steep banking at Brooklands enabled drivers to take the corners very fast. But those going too fast would fly over the top!

Parry moved in early in 1923, with his two dogs Togo and Bess, and straight away he started to do what he'd always wanted to do – build and race fast cars.

Ninety years ago cars were not raced in classes according to engine size as they are today. All cars, large or small, raced together. Sometimes a handicapping system would be used. Either cars had a few seconds deducted from their lap times according to their engine size, or slower cars were allowed to start before faster ones. It was often hard to tell who had actually won!

This made it difficult for car makers and companies who supplied oil, petrol, tyres and car accessories to advertise how good their products were, and how much better they were than their competitors.

The answer to this problem was to hold speed and reliability competitions for different classes of cars. Sponsorship money became available for anyone who could claim a national or world record, as well as free fuel, lubricants and spares. This would provide much-needed support for Parry Thomas's research and allowed him to throw himself completely into the work. In 1923 alone, he broke twenty British records and two world records, as well as winning seven races in his modified Leyland 8, against names such as Bugatti, Bentley and Mercedes Benz. Life became very busy for Parry Thomas, and very expensive.

1924 saw Parry Thomas continue his run of success in time trials and record-breaking. His original stripped-down Leyland 8, which he had started racing in 1922, gradually evolved through a re-bodied stage to a lowered and much modified Leyland Thomas No 1, and was joined by the Thomas Special.

However, things were changing fast.
A new challenge had been born –
the World Land Speed Record.
Everyone had to have a go.
Henry Segrave, a famous
American racing driver and
ex-fighter pilot, started
preparing a Sunbeam Tiger
to challenge for the title.

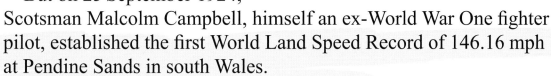

But on 25 September 1924,
Scotsman Malcolm Campbell, himself an ex-World War One fighter
pilot, established the first World Land Speed Record of 146.16 mph
at Pendine Sands in south Wales.

The following day
Parry Thomas looked at
the two cars in his
garage and knew neither
could match that speed.
He'd have to
go shopping.

The Birth of Babs

Now, you might have thought that Chitty Chitty Bang Bang was a made-up magical car from a children's film.

But what you might not know is that there were four of them and they were real. They couldn't fly, but they were fast. They didn't have wings but one of them had an engine from a fighter plane. They were owned by Count Zborowski, a rich Polish racing driver, almost 100 years ago.

In those days many cars had no silencers. Zborowski's 'Chittys' were in this category, and were so noisy that the local council passed a law banning him from the town!

Sadly, the Count was killed in a crash at the 1924 Italian Grand Prix. Parry Thomas managed to buy Chitty 4, the one with the fighter plane engine, from Zborowski's family for £125. He went straight to work on his new car.

Chitty 4 had a 27 litre aeroplane engine of 450 horsepower. Because it was made for an aeroplane it was light and reliable, but if he was going to break the Land Speed Record, Parry Thomas would need more power. By fitting special pistons and extra carburettors he managed to get 600 horsepower out of the big engine – 100 horsepower more than his nearest rival, Malcolm Campbell's Bluebird.

Parry Thomas then looked at Chitty's square shape and knew that it would create too much wind resistance, so he fitted a streamlined nose and tail and smooth wheel covers.

She was like a new car and would need a new name. What could it be? Parry Thomas was stuck, until the next day his favourite niece, Pamela, came to visit him in his workshop. Pamela's nickname was . . .

Meanwhile, Malcolm Campbell had not been idle. He knew that Henry Segrave was about to bid for the Land Speed title. So was Parry Thomas with his £125 second-hand banger, but Campbell wasn't too worried about him. He knew Bluebird's engine was good enough to break the record so, on 21 July 1925, Campbell raised his previous record, again on Pendine Sands, with an average speed of 150.869 mph.

Back at Brooklands, Parry Thomas, spurred on by Campbell's achievement, did even more work on Babs and on 19 October he was at Pendine. The weather was terrible. Sand, spray and high winds made it impossible to push Babs to her limit and he was forced to give up.

He loaded Babs onto the back of her lorry and headed for home.

Newspapers covered all the details of the various record attempts and the rivalry between the three drivers. They whipped up a frenzy of excitement in their readers. At last, at Christmas time 1925, Bluebird and Babs were put on display at the Schoolboys' Exhibition in London for all to see, with both drivers there to answer questions – but never at the same time!

Then, on 21 March 1926, at Southport Beach in the north-west of England, Henry Segrave broke Campbell's record with an average speed of 152.3 mph.

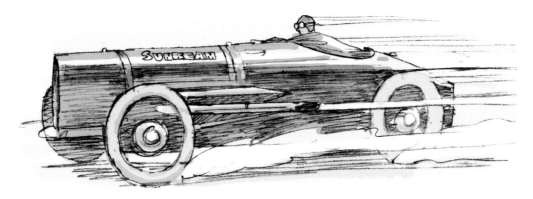

The time had come for Babs to show what she could really do.

The Land Speed Record

27 April 1926. A beautiful spring day at Pendine Sands. Perfect conditions. RAC (Royal Automobile Club) timing officials, mechanics, signallers, sponsors' representatives, police and doctors – fifty-three people in all – waited for Babs to make her run. With a mighty roar she sprang into life, but all was not well. She was misfiring badly and emitting clouds of black smoke. Parry Thomas quickly made adjustments to the engine. She wasn't quite right yet but he decided to go for it anyway.

This was to be an attempt on the 'flying mile', which meant he had to get Babs up to her maximum speed before he got to the first timing post. The second post was exactly a mile away and his speed would be measured between them. It came out at 168.074 mph, a new world record! Then next day, with another attempt, he broke his own record with 171.01 mph – twenty miles per hour faster than Bluebird's best.

Parry Thomas – Bus Driver

While all this had been going on, there had been great unrest in the country. The price of coal had fallen and mine owners decided to cut wages and increase the hours of miners to make up for it. The miners could not accept this and decided to call a strike. Other unions supported the miners and a general strike took place between 3 and 12 May 1926.

London bus drivers were among the strikers. Other people wanted to break the strike and some volunteered to drive buses, though they had to have a policeman with them. For Parry Thomas, driving a bus was only an opportunity to test the bus's performance to see how it might be improved.

As it happened, he was not a good bus driver. A lot of the time, he was concentrating so hard on the bus's performance that he didn't notice people waiting at the stops to get on!

His bus driving job soon came to an end, but not before he had earned £15 in wages, a great deal of money in those days.

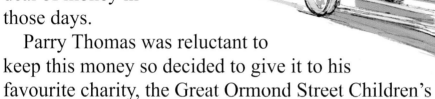

Parry Thomas was reluctant to keep this money so decided to give it to his favourite charity, the Great Ormond Street Children's Hospital. It cost £50 a year to sponsor a baby's cot at the hospital, more than many people could earn in a year at that time. Parry Thomas topped up his £15 with fees from radio broadcasts and public appearances. The cot he sponsored was named Babs. As well as this one, he sponsored another cot at the Belgrave Hospital for Children.

His generosity remained a secret to the public until after his death.

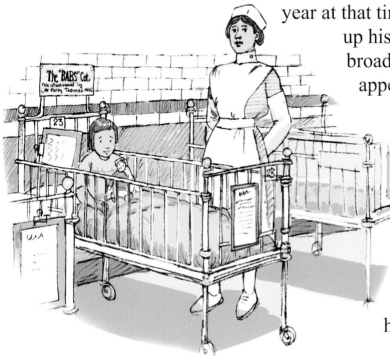

1927 – Disaster!

1 4 February: Campbell sets a new record . . . **174.22 mph!**

2 1 March: Segrave leaves by sea for Daytona Beach, USA, with his 1000 horsepower Sunbeam . . .

5 3 March: Pendine weather is bad. Thomas has 'flu but decides to run anyway.

6 Babs is fired up. Leslie Callingham, Thomas's technical advisor, and his mechanic, Jock Pullen, set off down the course in Callingham's Bentley.

8 The next thing they see is Babs, wrecked and on fire. Parry Thomas, horribly injured, is trapped in the car.

A campaign was launched by *The Autocar* magazine to sponsor the Babs cot at Great Ormond Street Hospital forever, in memory of Parry Thomas. Within eight weeks the target of £1,000 was reached and exceeded.

Babs Reborn!

Fast forward to 1969. Engineer Owen Wyn Owen decided that Babs was too important a piece of Welsh history to lie under Pendine Sands forever. There must be something there that could be put in a museum. To his surprise, when she was dug up, quite a lot of her was left.

Owen got to work in his garage. Bits that were beyond repair were re-made or sourced from original parts suppliers.

Sixteen years later, Babs flew down Pendine Sands once again.

To this day Babs can be seen every summer at the Museum of Speed in Pendine, Carmarthenshire.

For his good work and contribution to Welsh history, Owen Wyn Owen received the Tom Pryce Award in 1999.

You can read more about Tom Pryce on page 42 of this book.

ROBIN JAC EDWARDS

Early Days

For almost as long as Robert John Edwards, known as Robin Jac, could remember, there had been bikes and motorbikes for sale outside his parents' shop. Some were more like bicycles with engines and you still had to pedal uphill. Some were driven by leather belts and some had chains. Sometimes, late into the evening, he'd watch his dad fix motorbikes that had been brought in for repair.

One day in 1918, when he was aged eight, Robin hopped up on the saddle of a Velocette while his dad was having his tea. He had always been told not to play with the controls of the motorbikes. Of course, Robin didn't listen. He knew what every lever and switch was for on every motorbike in the shop.

His dad caught him on the bike and Robin quickly tried to hop off but his dad's face broke into a grin. He pushed the bike off its stand, swung his leg over and sat on the seat behind Robin. He pushed a few levers, jumped on the kick-starter and the bike roared into life.

At first Robin's dad worked the controls, but soon Robin was shifting the gears, letting out the clutch and advancing the spark, and his dad was little more than a passenger.

Then one day disaster struck. Coming home from school, Robin found his mother crying in the kitchen. Running to her side, he asked what was the matter. Robin's dad, who had suffered from ill-health for many years, had died.

Making Mischief

Everything changed from that day on. Robin's mother married again so he had a new dad. The family moved out to granddad's place, far away from Robin's friends. Soon, the bright but mischievous Robin was getting into all kinds of trouble.

Fortunately for Robin, a local headmaster started a motorcycle club so, instead of getting into mischief, he got back into what he loved most – motorbikes.

Down to Work

After leaving school and spending a brief time working in a bank in Llandudno, Robin decided to follow his heart and rented a small workshop in Llanuwchllyn where he started doing motorcycle repairs. Business boomed and soon he was repairing tractors and cars, too. When he started selling cars, he began to make more money. At last, he could afford to do something he'd always dreamed of – racing in the world's top motorbike event, the Isle of Man Tourist Trophy – the TT.

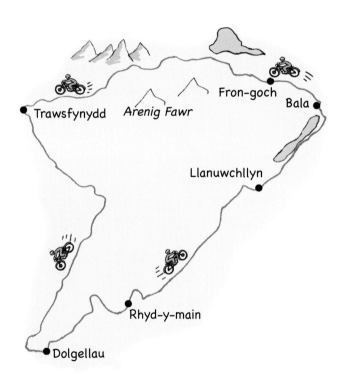

Robin had been in motorbike races in the Oswestry area but the TT was where the best in the world competed. He would have to do some serious practising. He knew that the roads that ran over the hills in his area were much like the roads on the Isle of Man. After studying a map of the TT course he came up with a 55-mile route that closely matched it.

It worked well, but to avoid the police he had to practise with his noisy racing motorbike very early in the morning. This led to problems with people trying to sleep in Trawsfynydd . . .

. . . sheep trying to sleep on the road . . .

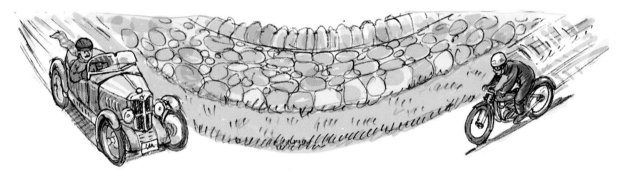

. . . and worst of all, cars suddenly appearing around blind bends!

But there was an answer. Lads from the local motorbike and cycling clubs agreed to act as lookouts and sheep chasers for Robin.

It worked, and soon Robin was ready to give the TT course a go.

Racing on the Isle of Man

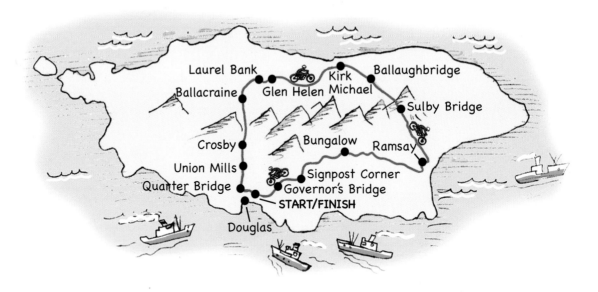

In the early 1900s, it was illegal to close roads in the UK for motor sport – and the speed limit was 20 mph. The Auto-Cycle Club, which was in charge of motorcycle events, knew that motorbikes would never improve without the tough testing of design and materials that comes with long-distance racing, as was happening in Europe. The Isle of Man, although part of the UK, had its own government with the power to make its own traffic laws. It still does. Government officials realised that running an annual race on the island might attract a lot of tourists – and their money. They were absolutely right.

Since 1907, the TT has been a world-class motorcycle event, with thousands of bikers and spectators arriving for a holiday every June. In the early days, the course was much shorter since the first motorbikes didn't have enough power to climb the mountains, or brakes good enough to stop them hurtling down the other side too quickly.

The race was run mostly on dirt roads, with the first rider having to open farm gates and the last rider through having to close them. Collisions with sheep and cattle were frequent. Boy Scouts had to stand by these obstacles and wave flags to warn riders of the dangers.

Since 1920, riders have had to cover a difficult 38 mile course around the island's twisty, stone-walled public roads. Over the last 100 years or so, racing bikes have changed beyond all recognition, due in large part to improvements brought about by the need to win races.

1912
• belt-driven
• no suspension
• rim brakes
• leather helmet
• tweeds

1920s
• chain-driven
• drum brakes
• crash helmet
• full leathers

1940s
• hydraulic shock absorbers
• megaphone exhausts

1950s
• full fairing

1970s
• hydraulic disc brakes
• full-face helmet

TODAY
• quad disc brakes
• carbon fibre full fairing
• sponsorship

Today, riders hurl their superbikes at speeds touching 200 mph through pretty villages and over mountains and moorland often shrouded in fog and lashed by rain.

The Grand Prix Years

By 1934, Robin Jac felt ready to tackle the most famous motorbike racing course in the world. As an amateur he had to compete in the Grand Prix races – the TT was only for professionals. On a warm Friday evening, in late May 1934, the ferry from Liverpool had just steamed into the harbour at Douglas, Isle of Man. On the car deck, as the big steel doors opened, sixty-four high-powered motorbikes were kick-started into life. Robin revved the engine of his Cotton and shot up the ramp, followed by riders from all over Europe.

Even before the swarm of excited bikers had reached the esplanade it looked a lot like a race, but before things got too out of hand, a burly policeman stepped into the road bringing them to a screeching halt.

All right, lads, that's enough. A few simple rules: no racing, no engine-revving off the course, no disorderly behaviour. Do I make myself clear?

Keeping the warning in mind, Robin rode slowly to the campsite. It was late when he put up his tent and because he had to practice at six o'clock in the morning, he had an early night.

But next morning, thick fog covered the the island. There would be no practice runs till it lifted, so instead, Robin studied a map of the course. Six laps of a thirty-eight mile mountain course. Wow!

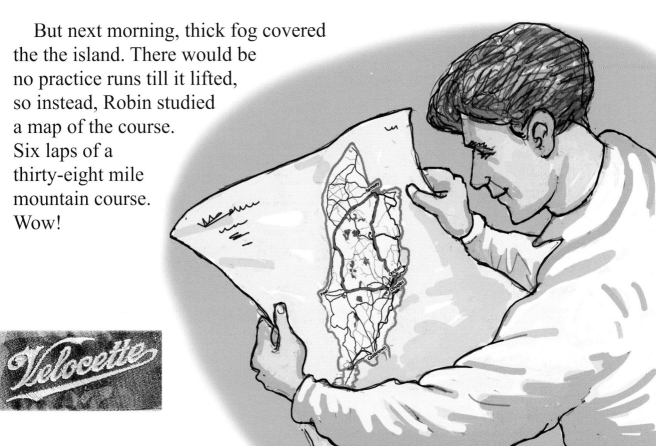

In the end, mechanical problems stopped Robin Jac from finishing the Grand Prix that year, but in 1935, he was back, this time with some helpers. Their job would be to stand at various points around the course equipped with placards and binoculars. They would let Robin know what his position in the race was as he roared past. This would be a great help since he would then know if he needed to go faster or not. But from a distance in the fog and rain how would they know it was him? Looking at the red dragon on his helmet, he had an idea – to paint his brown leathers red!

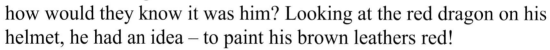

Anxiously, he waited at the start line as each rider set off at timed intervals. At last he was away.

... through Ballacraine

He did six laps at an average speed of 61 mph. It took him
3 hours 43 minutes to finish eighth among some of the best riders
in the world.

The TT at Last

After World War Two, when all racing had stopped, everyone was keen to get back in the saddle again. Robin was great friends with top Irish rider Stanley Woods, who won the TT ten times and the Manx Grand Prix 2 twenty-nine times. Woods owned a sweet factory and always made sure that the Boy Scouts who worked the scoreboards had several boxes, no doubt to keep them sweet!

The first race would be the Belgian Grand Prix. Robin was keen to give it a go and Woods very kindly lent him his Norton motorbike.

Robin was doing very well, and was in a good position to win, but two big crashes had left oil on the track and, before the stewards could clean it up, Robin skidded on it and had a terrible accident. His doctor said he must take a long rest but Robin ignored this advice and entered the Manx Grand Prix five weeks later, coming fourth despite not having fully recovered.

Then in 1949 Robin Jac turned professional in order to race in the TT. This would be the first year that it would be the official British round of the Road Racing World Championship and it attracted the world's best riders.

These riders had teams of mechanics and state-of-the-art motorbikes, with lots of financial backing to pay for the very latest equipment. The Moto Guzzi team was the greatest of these and dominated the TT in this period. Robin Jac had to do most of the work on his bike, which was nearly twenty years old, himself, with the help of one or two friends. He had to pay all his expenses out of his own income. Even so he came ninth ahead of twenty other riders.

Robin Jac's last race was in the 1950 TT, when he again came ninth ahead of many of the great riders of the day. With his great talent, he might have been placed much higher had he been a member of a team with mechanical and financial support. He could easily have become a racing hero to a much wider audience. But every time he stepped up on the podium his many fans sang the Welsh National anthem, 'Land of My Fathers'.

He died in 1979, aged 68.

TOM PRYCE

Boy Racer!

It was a Saturday morning in spring,
1957. Tom Pryce was eight years old.
In the front seat of his dad's car,
he was just waking up. It had been
a long drive to Oulton Park racing
circuit and even though Tom was
very excited, the early start had made
it hard for him to keep his eyes open.
"Are we nearly there yet?" Tom asked his dad
for the tenth time. At last the answer was:
 "Yes, we're there."

Tom rubbed his eyes in disbelief as he sat up and looked out.
All around them were parked the most beautiful sports cars Tom had
ever seen – new Triumph TR3s, Jaguar XK120s, Aston Martin DB3s
and many more. Tom had only ever seen these in magazines – and this
was just the car park!

Then he heard it for the first time in his life. The high pitched yelp of a racing engine. The excitement was almost too much to bear. Tom jumped from the car and ran through a gate into the pits. Dozens of high-powered racers were being revved up as mechanics did some last minute tuning. The noise was deafening. Tom loved it.

The racing started at one o'clock. Tom was wild with excitement as Lotuses, Coopers, Ferraris and Jaguars screamed past the rickety wooden fence.

By the end of the afternoon Tom knew what he wanted to be when he grew up – a racing driver.

From that day on Tom thought about cars all the time. His bedroom walls had posters of all his racing heroes and their cars – Stirling Moss, Graham Hill and Juan Manuel Fangio in their Mercedes Benz, Lotus and Ferrari cars.

Two years later, when he was aged ten, the local baker asked Tom if he would like to help deliver bread and cakes. It sounded like fun and Tom agreed. And when the baker showed Tom how to turn the van around in a field at the far end of the delivery run, Tom was in heaven.

At first he was very careful, but his confidence grew till one day, while the baker was talking to a customer, he though he might try and slide the car sideways around corners like he'd seen his heroes do at Oulton Park. It was great fun! Easy too, on the field's muddy surface.

Tom felt like a real hero – until the baker opened the back door of the van. Then he had to clean up the messy pile of bread and cakes that had landed on the floor.

Racing School

Tom hated school, but he stuck at it until he was sixteen, when he left to become an apprentice tractor mechanic. He didn't much like that either, but he did learn about engines. For four years he never lost sight of his dream to be a racing driver, and one day he saw a racing school advertisement in a car magazine. The school was in Mallory Park, Leicestershire.

Tom went for a trial and was accepted. This meant dividing his time between his job in Wales and the racing school. He was a good student, but was impatient with routine car maintenance. So, when other students were busy checking tyre pressures, suspension settings and brake adjustments, Tom would jump straight into the car and be off.

One day, Tom saw a poster in the school cafeteria advertising a series of car races run by a newspaper, with a first prize of a Formula Ford Lola race car. He had to win that car!

Race after race, Tom drove for all he was worth. Then came the day of the final race. Tom qualified on the third row of the grid – not a good place to start, and it was raining. All the other drivers were complaining about how hard it was going to be to keep the cars from sliding off the slippery track. Tom just smiled. Having grown up in north Wales, he wasn't afraid of driving in the rain, and driving a baker's van in a muddy field had been good training!

Tom Pryce won easily and he was now the proud owner of a real racing car. But where was he going to keep it? The answer was easy. In exchange for doing some work on the school's racing cars, Tom could keep his car in their garage and practise on the circuit whenever he wanted to.

Testing Times

Now that he was the proud owner of a new Lola, and with the Daily Express newspaper paying for oil, petrol and tyres, Tom Pryce decided it was time to give up his job at the tractor garage and become a full-time racing driver. The car had a place to stay at the school garage, but he didn't. Tom had heard of a boarding house near Brands Hatch. It was run by a kindly, but quick-tempered lady, called Mrs 'Red' Webb, who liked racing drivers and had several of them living there. Most of them were poor and sometimes could not pay their rent, but she was happy to wait until they won a race and could settle their bills.

Clean it up!

That's it! Had enough!

However, there was one thing Red couldn't stand and that was

rudeness. One evening, Tom was rushing to go out on a big date. He was running late and was in a bad mood. He made the mistake of saying that her food wasn't very good. Red tipped his dinner over his head. That was a mistake Tom never made again.

To pay for his race entry fees Tom would test new racing cars for Lotus and Lola at the major tracks – Silverstone, Snetterton and Brands Hatch.

Tom was the kind of driver who could take a car to its limits but he wasn't so good at analysing and describing its faults. However, he could always think of something to say.

A Professional Driver

Even though he was having a wonderful time racing in England, Tom Pryce missed Wales and also speaking Welsh. When he became lonely, he'd ring his father to come and pick him up and, after a noisy sprint up the motorway in his dad's Lotus Cortina, they would always stop at Tom's favourite spot near his home in north Wales – Clocaenog. After Brands Hatch, the peace and quiet did him good.

Peace, however, would be in short supply for Tom in 1971. A chance came up to race in open-wheel single-seater VW Beetles, known as Formula Vee. He started to win races and attract a lot of attention. It was time for him to move up the racing ladder.

VW Beetle

Formula 3 has always been the first step on the ladder to Formula 1. In 1971, the cars had a 1600cc rear engine, independent suspension and four-wheel disc brakes. They were like miniature Formula 1 cars.

Royale Racing Cars had been impressed with Tom's performances and gave him a tryout in their new F3 car. In his first outing for the team, he came third. About this time, his dad asked Tom to put five black bars on the front of his helmet so he could spot him in a race.

Tom didn't let Royale down. In the 1972 season opener at Brands Hatch, he outstripped the opposition, including big names of the day, such as James Hunt and Jochen Mass. Royale's team boss kept signalling him to slow down, but Tom just went faster. He was named the Royale F3 Driver of the Year.

Formula 1

Bad luck stalked Tom Pryce's next three F3 races. He was fast and impressive at both Oulton Park and Zandvoort, but didn't finish.

Then, at Monaco, his car stopped in Casino Square. Pryce tried to fix it at the side of the road but another driver smashed into his car, breaking his leg and throwing him through a shop window.

However, not even an accident like this could slow Pryce down. He was busier than ever, first winning the Formula Super Vee series, then four races in Formula Atlantic (slightly faster F3 cars). Soon, he came to the attention of someone who would be very important in the history of Formula 1, the man behind the world-beating McLaren team, Ron Dennis.

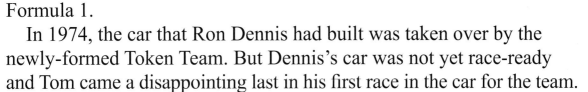

Dennis and his team, Rondel Racing, put Pryce in their F2 car where he did very well through 1973. And during this time, Dennis was building the car that was to be Pryce's first drive at the top of the motorsport world – Formula 1.

In 1974, the car that Ron Dennis had built was taken over by the newly-formed Token Team. But Dennis's car was not yet race-ready and Tom came a disappointing last in his first race in the car for the team.

The next few F1 races also fell short of expectations, so much so that the organisers of the Monaco Grand Prix wouldn't let Tom compete. They said he lacked experience – but he was determined to show them!

Nothing was going to stop Tom from racing at Monaco that year. When he was offered an F3 drive at the greatest road racing circuit in the world, he jumped at the chance.

He won by an amazing 20 seconds!
This astonishing victory got noticed and Tom was flooded with
offers from F1 teams. He finally went with the Shadow Racing Team.

Triumph – and Tragedy

Then, in 1975, came Tom Pryce's big day. It was his fourth F1 race of the season, held at Brands Hatch. There was rain and wind, and there were snow flurries, Pryce's favourite racing weather – just like home!

Tom has pole position. Although it's wet, he chooses slick tyres – all the better to slide with!

Jackie Ickx jumps into first place at the start. Three others overtake him. Scheckter leads. Jarier goes in for slick tyres. Tom is fourth!

Tom passes Peterson into third place. Then passes Ickx into second. Scheckter is twelve seconds ahead but slows down when he comes up behind slower cars.

Tom steadily reels Scheckter in. Lap 16, only five seconds behind him. Lap 20, three seconds.

⑤ Lap 25, Tom's right behind Scheckter.

Tom is pushing, pushing – until . . . Scheckter's engine gives up under the strain!

⑥

⑦ Tom went on to win.

Tom Pryce is the only Welshman ever to have won a Grand Prix. The rest of the season also went well, with pole position in the British Grand Prix, third place in the Austrian and fourth in the German.

However, changes in the required specification for the cars in the 1976 season caught the Shadow team unprepared and they struggled to change their design quickly enough to become competitive once again. Tom finished the year in twelfth place in the Drivers' Championship.

The beginning of 1977 looked better for the Shadow Racing Team. There was extra money from new Italian sponsors. However, Tom was forced to retire in the first two races due to mechanical problems.

The third race of the year was at Kyalami in South Africa . . .

With the death of Tom Pryce, Grand Prix racing lost a great driver who might have been the first Welsh World Champion.

Everyone who saw him race said he was a very skilled and fearless driver but sometimes, maybe, he was too brave for his own good. He was one of those drivers who either won, placed well, or wound up in the gravel. However, no-one was in any doubt that, as he gained experience, he would have been winning more and going off less.

Everyone who knew him also said he was a quiet, kind man and a good friend.

The Tom Pryce Trophy is awarded annually by the Welsh Motoring Writers group to the man or woman who they feel has contributed most to motoring or transport that year. In 1996, it was awarded to Gwyndaf Evans.

"Fe gurodd y goreuon heb gefnu ar ei gynefin"

On 11 June 2009, on what would have been his sixtieth birthday, a memorial plaque to Tom Pryce was unveiled in his home town of Ruthin, in north Wales. The inscription reads 'Fe gurodd y goreuon heb gefnu ar ei gynefin' ('He beat the best without forgetting his roots').

Gwyndaf Evans

Trainee driver

Gwyndaf Evans grew up with cars. His dad owned a garage in Dinas Mawddwy, north Wales, and sometimes if an old banger was too bad to fix, he would buy it for spares or scrap.

As soon as Gwyndaf could reach the pedals, his dad let him race the bangers around hay bales in his granddad's field, like racing drivers did at real race tracks in those days.

Gwyndaf dreamed of being a racing driver, so he practised sliding round the corners – 'drifting' – like real racers did. The bangers were always breaking down so, with a few tools, Gwyndaf soon learned how to get them going again.

By the time he was fifteen, he was sometimes left in charge of the garage when his parents went away for the weekend. Mostly, there wasn't much to do, so Gwyndaf would take his old Mini Traveller and practice doing handbrake turns around the petrol pumps.

He had seen rally drivers do this on gravel tracks in the forests near his home.

In high speed corners, they would yank at the handbrake, locking the rear wheels just as they turned the steering wheel to go into the corner. The back end would swing round quickly, leaving the car pointing in the right direction. Then the driver would quickly floor it and roar away in dramatic style! Even though he still wanted to be a racing driver this was something Gwyndaf wanted to learn.

Competition

When he turned sixteen, Gwyndaf felt he was ready to try some real motorsport – banger racing! The competitors were mostly other lads from the area who had access to tired old cars and a field to drive them in. All that was needed was a friendly farmer with land far enough away from houses, so noise wouldn't matter, plus a few hay bales and old tyres to mark the course.

At seventeen, Gwyndaf could at last drive on public roads in his old Mini Traveller. It was time to try something new – road rallying. These events, usually run by car clubs, would start at eleven o'clock at night and end at five o'clock in the morning, when the roads were quiet. They weren't races as such: the idea was to get from one checkpoint to another in an exact time. If you were late, or early, you would lose points.

Competitors would begin their runs at five minute intervals. The times for these stages, as they were called, were set so you never had to break the speed limit, but if you got lost or broke down and had to make up time, you would have to get a move on.

To compete in these events you needed a navigator to read maps, follow written directions, and make sure the driver wasn't going too slow or too fast.

Up until the 1960s, all rallying was like this. There were no full-time drivers who got paid to do it, and few specially-built rally cars. But gradually everything changed. Money flooded into the sport from TV and advertising. Television coverage demanded more action, so special stage rallying was born, and with it the professional paid rally driver. For Gwyndaf, rallying began to look like a career.

Special stage rallying in Britain mainly happens on gravel tracks in forests. The cars still have to travel between the stages in set times and seconds are deducted from their overall times for arriving late or early at a checkpoint. Once at the checkpoint the idea is to drive

the special stages, which can be several miles long, as fast as you can.

The driver and navigator drive the track beforehand, taking notes on every bend, dip and hill in the stage. These are called pace notes. Here are what some pace notes might look like.

long
4L   Flat R&L
70   Flat L long +Flat R long
              tight
      9L   Crest   long
         3R   L
            tight

Key:
4 = 40 degrees

Long = a long corner

Flat = flat out, top speed

Tight = a sharp corner

Crest = top of a hill

L = left

R = right

On the day of the rally, the navigator reads back the pace notes just as the corners and dips come up. That way, the driver can concentrate on going as fast as he can, sometimes getting the car ready for a bend that he can't even see yet.

Through the 60s and 70s rally cars became more specialised as manufacturers realised the sales potential of a rally win. Soon, there were very expensive, specially built rally cars competing, such as the Lancia Stratos, and Audi Quattro, and heavily modified family cars like the Ford Escort RS 1600 and Mini Cooper S.

Studded snow tyres for Monte Carlo Rally

Rear wing for high speed stability

Air dam for reduced wind resistance

Lightweight body panels

Heavy duty bull bars for African Rally

Spotlights for high speed night driving

Teams also began to use highly skilled mechanics to service the more complex cars. Drivers did not have to get their hands dirty.

Interiors became more like aircraft cockpits, and the cost of a competitive rally car grew and grew.

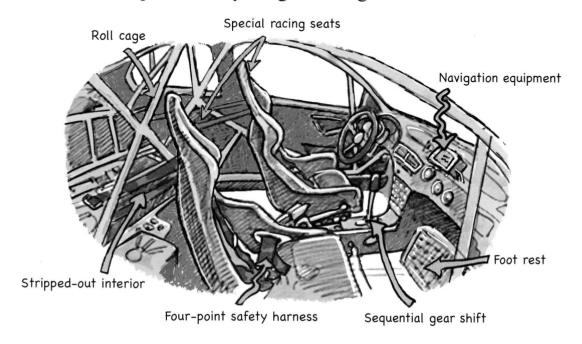

Roll cage

Special racing seats

Navigation equipment

Stripped-out interior

Four-point safety harness

Sequential gear shift

Foot rest

Gwyndaf gets going

Meanwhile, Gwyndaf was enjoying small local rallies. Family and friends helped him prepare his cars, which were mostly old ones. His dad's garage, Evans Motors, sponsored his first rally cars – a Mini, a Mazda RX3, a Ford Escort Mk2 and a Toyota.

Gwyndaf's reputation as a fast driver grew, and he was able to attract the bigger and better sponsorship which was necessary to compete in major UK rallies.

In 1986, Gwyndaf managed to buy a very special Sierra Cosworth, one of only seven built by Ford. He drove it three times in the Lombard RAC Rally, and won the Group N class in the 1988 British Rally championship. Although second-hand, this was one very quick car, turbo-charged with 275 horsepower. Sierras like this can cost up to £40,000 even today.

In 1989 he drove another Ford Sierra which was not his own this time . . .

. . . to win the Ulster Rally – in spite of the awful colour!

Soon the young Welshman was spotted by Ford's competition department. They offered him a job as a rally and test driver. At last, starting in 1990, Gwyndaf would be paid for what he loved doing best – driving fast cars.

With Ford sponsoring him for the next eight years, Gwyndaf competed in the World Rally Championships against some of the best drivers on the planet in many exciting countries.

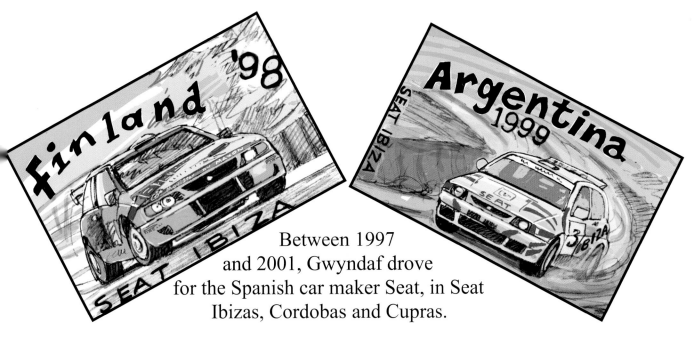

Between 1997 and 2001, Gwyndaf drove for the Spanish car maker Seat, in Seat Ibizas, Cordobas and Cupras.

Next, four years rallying with MG in their ZR1600. Then, back in the UK, with Mitsubishi from 2004 to 2010.

Oops!

Rally driving can be fun but sometimes it can also be dangerous. In a foreign country, in extreme weather, it can be easy to make a bad mistake. Gwyndaf Evans made two of them in Sweden.

First mistake

A rally stage, late afternoon, very cold. An easy right hand bend, but something went wrong. Instead of a controlled, high-speed power slide on studded tyres, Evans and his  co-driver found themselves upside down. Both unhurt, they signalled to the spectators to come and push the Sierra back on its wheels. "En, två, tre, vräka!" shouted the enthusiastic crowd as they heaved the heavy car back up.

Everything seemed fine, but the safety glass in the windscreen was crazed over. Gwyndaf couldn't see a thing. He frantically signalled the crowd to smash out the windscreen. The excited lads didn't need to be asked twice. In seconds, the Cozzie was on its way again at high speed. It didn't take long for Gwyndaf to realise his mistake. The temperature outside was -20C. At 60 mph with wind chill this is equivalent to -62C. They would have frostbite in five minutes. Their rally was over.

Second mistake

Practising on icy roads late at night. After taking a huge jump, the car stopped. Gwyndaf knew they were low on fuel, so assumed that must be the reason. He and his navigator started walking. They had been warned not to stay out later than nine o'clock because the weather was dangerously cold.

After collecting some fuel from a farmhouse some miles away, shivering and hungry, Gwyndaf lifted the boot lid to pour in the petrol. Then he noticed – the problem wasn't lack of fuel after all. The impact of the jump had jolted the emergency ignition switch to the 'off' position. All that way for nothing – and they might have frozen to death!

Building a Rally Car

Rally cars may look like a normal car, but underneath, almost everything is different. When a car maker like Ford or Seat decide to build a rally car, they will take one off the production line and remove everything so that only the shell remains. Gwyndaf Evans' Seat would have looked like this.

Inside this shell, they will build a very strong 'rollcage' made of tubular steel to protect the driver in case of a bad accident. The cage also joins all four corners of the car where the wheels are connected so, even if the car hits something hard, the body won't get bent out of shape and be impossible to steer.

In a normal car the body panels, roof, wings and sills are only 'tacked' together, with spaces in between spot welds. In a rally car, the welds are continuous, making the car stronger still.

The wheels in a normal car are all connected to springs, hubs and shock absorbers, which make up the suspension. This is all replaced in a rally car by a suspension made of a strong, light materials of the

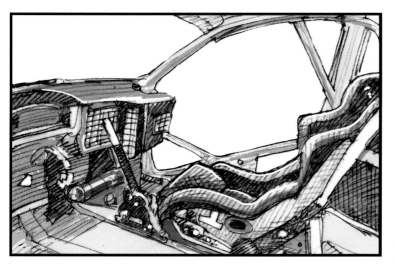

same quality used in aircraft. It has to be very strong to withstand the high-speed jumps and bumps that these cars have to endure thousands of times in every rally. Like important aircraft parts, the suspension components are replaced at regular intervals whether they are broken or not.

Even the steering is modified to suit the driver. Gwyndaf Evans likes light steering, but his team-mate might not. The special racing seat is made to fit a particular driver, to hold him in tightly when taking high-speed corners.

Extra-strong seat belt harnesses, with more straps, are also fitted to hold the driver in if the car rolls over. These, plus the rollcage, allow the driver and navigator to walk away from terrible crashes. The engine too, although it is basically the same as in a normal car, is tuned by race engineers to give much more power.

Home Ground

Gwyndaf Evans has now retired from international rallying but he still enjoys competing in UK events, especially classic rallying in old rally cars. With modern rally cars costing up to £500,000 and other costs coming to £100,000 per season, this is a good way to have all the fun of rallying at much lower cost. Some classic rally cars are almost as fast as their modern counterparts.

In 2009, Gwyndaf competed in six classic car rallies and won four! By halfway through 2010, he had already won the Jim Clark Rally and come second in the Isle of Man Rally. When he was competing internationally, he would often be away from Wales for nine months of the year. Now he doesn't do that, he can concentrate on having fun in other ways – racing a Lotus Elise at Silverstone Race Track, for example . . .

. . . or testing a very special MG estate car at 176 mph . . .

Parachute

. . . and trying not to worry when the braking parachute doesn't open!
   But most of all Gywndaf enjoys teaching his son, Elfyn, how to get the most out of his rally driving.

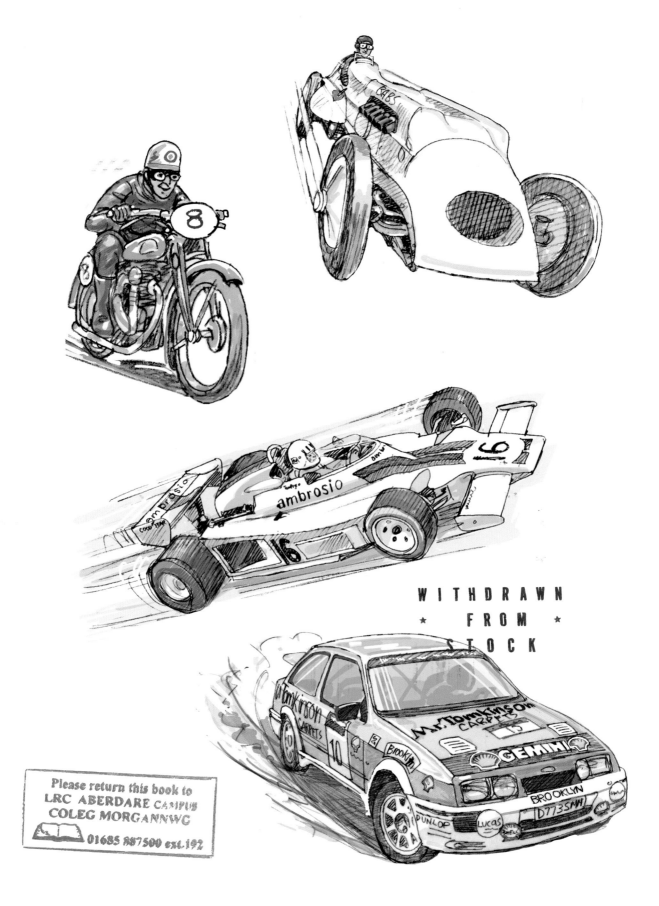